The Plymouth Thanksgiving

written and illustrated

by

Leonard Weisgard

DOUBLEDAY

NEW YORK LONDON TORONTO SYDNEY AUCKLAND

PASSENGERS ON THE MAYFLOWER

John Carver, his wife Katherine Carver, Desire Minter,
2 servants John Howland and Roger Wilder,
a boy William Latham, a maid servant, and a child Jasper More.

William Brewster, his wife Mary Brewster,
2 sons Love and Wrestling
and a boy Richard More and his brother.

Edward Winslow, his wife Elizabeth Winslow,
2 servants George Soule and Elias Story,
a little girl Ellen, sister of Richard More.

William Bradford and his wife Dorothy.

Isaac Allerton, his wife Mary Allerton,
their children Bartholomew, Remember and Mary,
a servant boy, John Hooke.

Samuel Fuller, and a servant William Butten.

John Crakston and his son John Crakston.

Captain Myles Standish and his wife Rose.

Christopher Martin, his wife,
2 servants Solomon Prower and John Langmore.

William Mullins, his wife Alice, 2 children Joseph and Priscilla,
a servant Robert Carter.

William White, his wife Susanna, a son Resolved
and one son born on the Mayflower called Peregrine,
2 servants William Holbeck, Edward Thomson.

Stephen Hopkins, his wife Elizabeth,
2 children by a former wife Gyles and Constance,
2 more children by this wife Damaris and Oceanus, born at sea,
2 servants Edward Doty and Edward Leister.

Richard Warren

John Billington, his wife Eleanor, 2 sons John and Francis.

Edward Tilley, his wife Ann,
2 children Henry Samson and Humility Cooper

John Tilley, his wife, and Elizabeth their daughter.

Francis Cooke and his son John.

Thomas Rogers and his son Joseph.

Thomas Tinker and his wife and son.

John Rigdale and his wife Alice.

James Chilton, his wife, and Mary their daughter.

Edward Fuller, his wife, and their son Samuel.

John Turner and 2 sons.

Francis Eaton, his wife Sarah, and their son Samuel.

Moses Fletcher, John Goodman, Thomas Williams,
Degory Priest, Edmund Margeson, Peter Brown,
Richard Britterige, Richard Clarke, Richard Gardiner,
Gilbert Winslow.

John Alden, hired as cooper.

John Allerton and Thomas English, hired.

William Trevore and one named Ely, hired.

The Plymouth Thanksgiving

PUBLISHED BY DOUBLEDAY   a division of Bantam Doubleday Dell Publishing Group, Inc. 666 Fifth
Avenue, New York, New York 10103   D O U B L E D A Y and the portrayal of an anchor with a dolphin are trademarks
of Doubleday, a division of Bantam Doubleday Dell Publishing Group, Inc.   Library of Congress Catalog Card Number
76-15379   ISBN 0-385-26754-1 (pbk.)   ISBN 0-385-26753-3 (lib. bdg.)   Copyright © 1967 by Leonard Weisgard
All Rights Reserved   Printed in the United States of America
9 10 11 12 13 14 15 16   (lib. bdg.)
1 2 3 4 5 6 7 8 9 10   (pbk.)

In England over 300 years ago
there lived some people called Pilgrims.

They were not happy
with the laws of the King
or the Church of England.
They were not allowed
to pray as they chose.
They were not allowed
to practice their faith.

The Pilgrims decided to leave England
and for a time they settled in Holland.

At that time an English explorer, Captain John Smith,
and other explorers and traders were charting new lands.
Stories of their exploration
had reached the Pilgrims in Holland.

There were stories of great fertile lands across the Atlantic,
stories of Indians, some friendly, some warlike,
of good hunting, of abundant fish,
of great bounty waiting there for new settlers.
Hearing this the Pilgrims decided to return to England
to make plans to settle
in the New World across the ocean.
There they might really be free!

From England
out of Plymouth Harbor
westward toward the New World
a little ship, the Mayflower,
got under way.

The month was September
in the year of our Lord, 1620.

One hundred and two passengers were on board.
John Carver, William Bradford,
and William Brewster
were the Pilgrim leaders.

Master of the ship
was Christopher Jones,
with two master's mates,
four petty officers,
one boatswain,
one surgeon
one gunner,
one cook,
and about twenty seamen
in the crew.

Down in the ship's hold
was furniture,
a ship's cat,
a mastiff, a spaniel,
and many supplies:
Farm tools, seeds,
barrels of beer,
pickled beef, pork or salthorse,
peas, beans, and a ship's biscuit
called hardtack.

And for arms
there were muskets,
powder and shot.

The ship's boat was on the upper deck
and stowed below
was another boat, called a shallop,
to be used for shallow water exploring.

For sixty-five days
and sixty-five nights
over a vast and furious ocean,
the Pilgrims journeyed
in the season of westerly gales.

Waves taller than houses
tossed the boat about.
Winds heaved it
from side to side.
The Mayflower rolled
and pitched,
buffeted every which way.

Passengers and crew
were badly shaken.
Some were ill.
One, William Butten,
died.

While still at sea,
a son was born
to Elizabeth and Stephen Hopkins.
Oceanus Hopkins
was his name.

On the morning
of the 11th of November,
when it seemed as though
this voyage would never end,
a voice called
from aloft:

"LAND HO!"

They all fell thankfully
to their knees.

God be praised.
He had delivered them safely.

Into the waters of the Atlantic,
off Cape Cod,
the Mayflower
dropped anchor.

Before the Pilgrims
set foot onto new soil
they met below
in the cabin
of the Mayflower.

A paper was prepared.
It was called
The Mayflower Compact.
Forty-one men signed
their names to it,
and took an oath.

In the name of God
they all agreed
to build a new colony.

The Pilgrims
would now be free
to practice their faith
and to pray
as they chose.

They all swore
to obey their Governor
and to keep the laws
for the good of all.

Now, to settle in the New World
a proper harbor must be found.
A harbor deep enough
for the Mayflower,
and larger boats as well.
Cleared land, timber,
and fresh water were needed too.
And a place
fitting and safe
from animals and Indians.

On the 15th of November
sixteen well-armed men led by Myles Standish,
lowered the ship's boat.
The shallop, battered in the rough crossing,
required mending before it could be used.

Once ashore
the explorers beached their boat.
They frightened some Indians
and a skinny dog.
But when the explorers tried to follow,
they were soon lost
in thickets and brambles.

The men grew thirsty.
Finding a spring they drank
their first fresh water in the new land.
In a clearing they found a corn field,
an Indian grave,
and an abandoned dwelling.
They found an iron kettle
and some Indian corn in baskets.

The second day was cold and rainy.
William Bradford slipped
and fell into an Indian deer trap.
Myles Standish and the men released him.

The land was barren and sandy.
Wet, discouraged, and scratched by briars
the group agreed this was no place to settle.
They returned to the Mayflower.

Life was bleak and hard.
Crowded on board the Mayflower
the Pilgrims found living difficult.
Some were feverish.
Those who were well enough
cared for those who were ill.
Food, drinking water, and supplies
dwindled fast.

The women washed and mended clothes.
They prayed and hoped
that very soon the men
would find a proper place
for settling.

On the 28th day of November
the shallop was ready and repaired.
This time Master Christopher Jones
with thirty-four well-armed men
sailed past the first landing place to a further shore.

For two days the group explored.
They shot geese and ducks for food.

They found two abandoned Indian dwellings.
And baskets of corn, beans, and tobacco.

And praise be to the Lord,
they found seeds enough
to plant the next spring!
When they were settled
the Pilgrims would return
to repay the Indians for what they had taken.

Six inches of snow fell.
Again the explorers
were discouraged and disappointed.
There was not much fresh water.
There was no proper harbor.
This was not a good place for a colony.
The men returned to the Mayflower.

It was now the month of December.
And the Pilgrims still had found
no land suitable for their new home.

The need to find a settling place
was greater than ever.
This time, all the Pilgrim leaders,
two mates, and a gunner
set forth again
in the shallop.

The weather was freezing.
The water blocked with ice.

Coming toward land they saw
Indians cutting up a fish.
They sailed two leagues farther
and then pulled to shore.

Some went to explore by land;
some explored by water.
And they all met together
in the evening.

Gathering brush and logs
they built a barricade.
Then they slept.

In the night there was a hideous cry.
Was it a wolf?
One man fired his musket.

All was still.

They rose at five.
While breakfasting one man shouted:

"INDIANS! INDIANS!"

Arrows whizzed past.
The explorers rushed
to the beach for their guns.
Muskets were shot.
Splinters of tree bark flew about.

But it pleased God to save them all.

The Indians fled.
No one,
no Indian nor Pilgrim,
was hit or harmed.

The men gave God thanks
and praise for their deliverance,
and named that place
"First Encounter Beach."

Weary from the battle,
the men trudged back
to the shallop.
They carried with them
bundles of arrows as souvenirs.

As the shallop moved away from shore
the sky grew black.
Snow and rain fell,
the wind howled,
the sea churned.

Suddenly the boat's rudder
snapped.
The crew was forced to steer
with oars.

As the winds grew wilder
the waves grew higher.
The mast of the shallop split.
The sail fell overboard.
Now with all their might
the men tugged on their oars.

They rowed and rowed.
The nighttime sky was black.
Finally they found their way
into the lee of a small island.

One seaman recalled the map
of Captain John Smith.
He had heard before of Plymouth Harbor.
Could this be it?

Here the group gathered wood.
They built a fire
and spent the night
huddled around it.

Next day was the Sabbath,
the 10th of December,
thanks be to the Lord.
It was a day of sunshine,
a Sunday of rest.

And across from the island
they could see what they
hoped was Plymouth.

On Monday, the 11th,
refreshed and restored
the explorers rowed
toward the mainland.
God be praised!
Taking soundings
the settlers found the water
deep enough for a fine harbor.
Not only for the Mayflower
but for larger boats as well.

On land they found
fresh water,
enough for a colony;
trees and forests,
wood enough for building,
and land already cleared,
where once Indians had lived.
The Pilgrim Fathers decided
here was where
they would settle.
They returned to the Mayflower
as quickly as they could.
They had found their homeland!

On the 15th day of December
Master Christopher Jones
ordered the ship's anchor raised.
And on the 16th day of December,
when the winds turned fair,
the Mayflower sailed across
to rest safe in Plymouth Harbor.

It was now the dead of winter.
A time of great struggle.

As soon as they could
the settlers planned a road
and began the building of their town.
They began to build their first
house for common use.

The earth was frozen.
The winds were cruel.
How very hard it was
to be a settler
in a New World.

Elder Brewster and Myles Standish
did much to nurse the sick.
But half the Pilgrim company died.

And as they buried their dead
they prayed and wondered.

Would this winter ever pass?

Ice began to melt,
the winter did pass.
Water ran from the earth.
Fish hawks called
and flew overhead.
And as the sun grew warm
there rose the fragrant
tangy smell of pine.

One day in March
an Indian came boldly
to the settlement.

He came in peace.
In broken English
he spoke to them.
How very surprised
the explorers were!

He told them
his name was Samoset.
He came from Monhegan,
a place far to the north.

From men who had come before,
he had learned English.
He told them of another Indian,
named Squanto,
who spoke even better English.
He told them of the great
Chief Massasoit, who soon
would visit the settlers.

The sun rose bright and warm.
on the 22nd day of March.
From out of the west,
silently, in Indian file,
sixty-two Wampanoags
approached Plymouth Colony.

Chief Massasoit was splendidly dressed.
Paint was stippled on his face.
Goosegrease made his hair shine.
He wore mooseskin moccasins,
deerskin leggings,
and a squirrel coat,
with the fur on the inside.
Bone beads hung around his neck.
Strapped to his coat was a knife.
And a tomahawk was in his hand.

When the Indians reached
the Pilgrim stockade
Chief Massasoit raised his hand.
Sixty-one Wampanoag Indians stood still.
One Indian, named Squanto,
called out loud and clear,
in a fine English accent:

"WELCOME ENGLISHMEN!"

Edward Winslow, the Governor's secretary,
went to greet the Indians.

Mr. Winslow bowed.
Then he escorted Chief Massasoit
and Squanto into an unfinished house.

He invited them to sit on pillows
upon a carpet on the floor.
He gave them gifts,
beads, a knife, some biscuits
and some butter.

Suddenly a trumpet blared.
Drums sounded.
Six men presented arms.

In came Governor Carver.
With great dignity
he bowed low
and kissed the hand
of the Indian Chief.
And he sat with them
on the floor.

They ate and drank
and talked together.

Squanto spoke while
Massasoit nodded and agreed.

"For as long as the moon rises,
for as long as the grass grows green,
for as long as the rivers flow,
we will be friends.
We will live in peace."

And so a treaty was made.

From that time on,
Squanto remained
to live with the Pilgrims
in Plymouth Colony.

Squanto was able to teach
the settlers many things,
Things that helped them to live
in this New World.

Squanto taught them
to watch for the bud of the white oak
to grow to the size of a mouse's ear.
To know then it is time to plant
corn in rows.
To set three herrings
at each corn hill,
to make the corn grow well.

He taught them to hoe with quahog shells.
To stalk deer with bow and arrow.
To dig in the mud for clams.
To look for eels and scallops.
And to boil a chowder
made of all these things.

Squanto taught the Pilgrims
to know which plants were good to eat
and which were poisonous.
Some were used for medicine, to heal the sick.

Squanto knew how to find groundnuts
and the roots of wild bean.
He taught them to know where berries grew best.
To broil roe over open fires.
To boil succotash and bake corn bread.
To refine sugar from the maples.

He taught them many things.

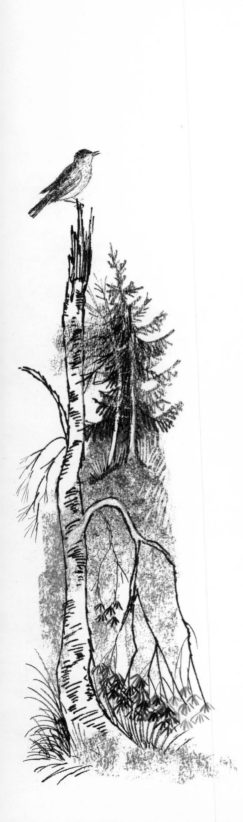

Working in the fields one day,
Governor John Carver
collapsed and died.

With a tribute of guns
and proper prayers
the Pilgrims buried him.

William Bradford, 31 years old,
was elected to be the new Governor.

The sun grew warmer.
Birds sang in the trees.
Wild flowers bloomed.
Hope grew high.
The sick grew well.

On the 12th day of May
in the year of our Lord 1621
there was a wedding.
The first in Plymouth Colony.
Edward Winslow married Susanna White.

Summer came.
The bees droned.
The Pilgrims worked hard.
It was a fruitful time,
a time of plenty.

The settlers grew well and strong.
And from the heavens,
and the earth, and the sea
God gave them bounty.
Pilgrim gardens grew and flourished.

While some explored,
others hunted,
some trapped,
others fished.
There was food enough for all
and more besides.

When the sun burned hot in July
Governor Bradford sent Mr. Winslow
and Mr. Hopkins to pay a friendly visit
to Chief Massasoit and his Indians.
Squanto went along
to show the way.

It was a long walk.
Forty miles to Mt. Hope,
where the Wampanoags lived.

There in front of his Indian house
sat the Indian Chief.
He swatted flies
and wore his squirrel coat.
This time, the fur
was on the outside.
On his head was a chief's hat
of turkey feathers.

Everyone sat down together
and talked.
Because they were all friends
they smoked each a turn from one pipe.
The smoke rose high.

And afterwards they played a game
of dice, called Hubbub.

Shadows grew long
and purple.
It was time for sleep.
Everyone stretched out
in the Indian wigwams.

It was not comfortable.
The visitors were bitten
by insects.

With the dawn's first light
and the first bird call,
Mr. Winslow, Mr. Hopkins,
and Squanto rose quietly.
Tired, hungry,
aching and bug-bitten
they hurried for home.

The days soon grew shorter.
Summer faded.
Leaves reddened.
Pumpkins grew fat,
orange and round.
The air was fragrant
with ripening fruit
and wood smoke.

Now was the time of harvest.
It was time to think of storing
food and supplies for the winter.

Corn was shucked and stacked.
Fruit was gathered in;
vegetables stored in houses.
Cod was salted.
Meat was cured.

Governor Bradford sent out men.
They shot ducks, geese, and quail.
They shot round plump turkeys.
There was food enough to share.

For three days
the women cooked.
The women baked.
The women worked and prepared.
And the children helped.

Tables were prepared
out of doors
alongside rough-hewn benches.
Fires blazed.

Governor Bradford sent a message.
Chief Massasoit, his Indian braves,
squaws and children
were all to come to Plymouth Colony,
to share a Thanksgiving feast.

When the day of the feast arrived,
so did the Indians.

Some in feathers.
Some in furs.
Some in animal skins.

Ninety-one Indians came,
braves, squaws and children
and some dogs besides.

As their contribution
to the feast,
Massasoit presented
five freshly killed deer
to the Pilgrims.

The deer were barbecued
over the roaring fires.
The tables were laden with food.
The air was fragrant
with the good smell of cooking.

There were clams and eels
and scallops and chowder.
There was game and fish and fowl.
There were nuts and berries and succotash.
There was corn bread and maple sugar.

There was food enough for all
and enough food to store
for the winter to come.

When the Pilgrims bowed their heads,
Indian squaws, braves
and children as well
listened to the prayers.

They thanked God
for carrying them across the seas.
For seeing them through the cruel winter.
For their Indian friends.
For the fruits of the earth.
For at last giving them a place
where they were free to worship
and to pray as they chose.

And everyone began to eat.

About the author-artist and this book

Leonard Weisgard is one of the foremost artists in the field of children's books. He began his career as a children's book illustrator at the age of twenty and by now he has well over 150 books to his credit. Among them is *The Little Island* by Golden MacDonald, which was awarded the 1947 Caldecott Medal.

Because facts about the Pilgrims and the story leading up to their first Thanksgiving are open to question, a great deal of research has been done in preparing this book. The text is based on information from William Bradford's detailed and interesting diary. The dates used are the same as the dates used by Bradford. These are old-style calendar dates which are ten days in advance of the calendar we now use. For clarity and consistency modernized place-names and names of people are used instead of the old-fashioned spelling of Bradford.

To make certain the illustrations would be as accurate as possible, Mr. Weisgard spent time at Plymouth, Massachusetts. This book has evolved with the generous assistance of both the Plymouth Antiquarian Society and the Plymouth Plantation Corporation, their research materials and artifacts, the re-creation of the Mayflower now in Plymouth Harbor and the restoration of the early settlement.